Bob

Be You!

Blessings

Richmore   Love,
                  Debbie

Praise for
Changing Your Heart

My wife and I have been married for almost 20 years. This book is a tremendous resource that will help rekindle your relationships using the strategies in this book.

Patrick Snow, International best-selling author of
Creating Your Own Destiny

The testimonies which follow Richmond and Debbie Caldwell's ministry are numerous. My wife and I have been touched deeply by the love and compassion manifested in their ministry to married couples and those seeking relational healing.

Parkey Cobern, Senior Pastor, Capstone Church

This book saved my marriage. I did not want another divorce.

Chris and Donellyn Dominguez, Firefighter and Midwife

This book will empower you to be able to communicate and understand your spouse better than ever.

Jim and Miki Aaron, Sales Manager and Office Asst.

The teaching had us ask the right questions of each other. It caused us to really listen to each other. It is all about trust.

Don Girard, Retired Army First Sergeant.

Richmond and Debbie are people of great character and integrity, but also of great imagination and humor. My wife and I are grateful beneficiaries of this book and their compassionate coaching.

Steve Cypher, Nuclear Power Plant Instructor

Many marriages in crisis have been genuinely touched and profoundly healed by the Lord through this delightful couple's ministry. Whether you need major assistance or just a tune-up, trust this wise teaching for sincere and effectual instruction.

Michael and Debbie Landis, Information Technology
Analyst and Homemaker

Our marriage was in trouble because it lacked a foundational platform necessary to sustain any healthy relationship. We were incapable of allowing our relationship to mature. Richmond and Debbie were instrumental in providing us with anointed Spiritual wisdom (instruction), caring and nurturing which has allowed us to grow in Christ and with each other.

Reggie and Charlotte Williams, Police Officer and
E.R. Technician

Today's world can create a hectic lifestyle. This marriage class enabled us to focus on each other rather than the busy details life throws at you. We laughed and we cried through this program that ultimately resulted in a stronger marriage.

Shannon and Maria Butler, Youth Director
and Super-Mom

Our prayer time together has increased and a paradigm shift has taken place in our lives. We now make sure our children see and hear our personal exchange and we have used the relational tools to strengthen our relationship with them.

Carl and Becky Everett, Engineer and Homemaker

Richmond helped me rebuild the marriage I broke.

Scott Cook, Firefighter

When my husband John told me that we should take the marriage course taught by Richmond and Debbie I asked him what was wrong with our marriage. He told me nothing was wrong he just thought it could be better. After taking this class it is! Now we've been blessed to be facilitators as well, mentored by the Caldwell's, and our marriage has gotten richer, deeper and better over the past four years!

John and Wynde Specht, Surveyor and Homemaker

A BLUEPRINT FOR STRONG MARRIAGES

CHANGING
YOUR HEART

HOW TO ENHANCE, REKINDLE, RESTORE
AND REPAIR YOUR RELATIONSHIPS

Richmond and Debbie Caldwell

AVIVA
PUBLISHING

NEW YORK

Changing Your Heart

How to Enhance, Rekindle, Restore and Repair Your Relationships

Richmond and Debbie Caldwell
RANDD Enterprises
6080 South Hulen St 360, PMB 209
Fort Worth, TX 76132
817-292-1120
www.ChangingYourHeart.com

ISBN: 978-1-890427-62-7

Library of Congress Control Number: 2008932786

Editor: Jeannine Mallory
Jacket Design: Shiloh Schroeder Design
Typesetting: Kimberly Martin

Every attempt has been made to properly source all quotes.
Printed in the United States of America
First Edition

Aviva Publishing
2301 Saranac Avenue, Ste. 100
Lake Placid, NY 12946
518-523-1320

DEDICATION

We dedicate this book to God who has blessed us, walked with us and given us the talent we have to write Changing Your Heart.

We dedicate this book to our children, who have gone through nights and weekends watching us take over the computer. Thank you for sticking with us.

To our parents, Richmond and Ursula Caldwell and Eugene and Janet Terry. Both couples have been married more than 50 years and are an inspiration. They always believed in us and spoke life-giving words along the way. We are truly grateful to you.

To our brothers and sisters, thanks for all the encouragement along the way.

To you, the reader: We pray that your life will be touched and that you will experience a true ***Change of Heart*** in all of your relationships.

ACKNOWLEDGMENTS

Many people encouraged, pushed and prompted us to write this book. Our foremost acknowledgement goes to Shannon Atkinson for his kind words, encouragement and behind-the-scenes help. Next are our Sam Camp teams, the Dream Achievers and the Goal Tenders.

Thank you, Patrick Snow for leading our journey through the publishing maze.

For Susan Friedmann, editor Jeannine Mallory, layout Kimberly Martin, web designer Tony Wall, jacket design Shiloh Schroeder and Sheridan printing, we thank you for envisioning our dream.

To Capstone Church, all of our family and friends who worship with us.

To Tabernacle of Praise for allowing us to spread our wings and share and teach.

To Tina for all your prayers, covering for us all the time and taking the kids whenever we needed you.

To Pastor Parkey and Rhonda Cobern, Pastors Gary and Toni Oliver, Pastor Renae Walker, Jerry and Connie

Sublett, Brad and Melba Burke, Jimmy and Miki Aaron, Michael and Debbie Landis, Ernest and Beverly Wade, The 'Heidelpeople,' Ron and Edna Jordan, Rick and Sylvia Hubbard, Dr. David and Teresa Ferguson, Bruce Walker, Jimmy Evans, K&A, Bobby Minor, Pastor Jeff and Cathy Wickwire, Frank and Eleanor Alfrido, Pat Murden, Merri-jo Hilaker and the hundreds of students who have participated in our workshops, coaching and seminars.

Thank you and bless you all!

TABLE OF CONTENTS

INTRODUCTION

Our Vision

We see the pain in our society. It is the result of broken relationships between family members, husbands and wives and friends. This pain is the result of people not yielding to each other and ingesting the intoxicating drug of always having to be right. We wrote this book to help and encourage you to see the possibility of change in your relationships by experiencing healing in your heart.

Our dream is to assist you in restoring your relationships. Do you feel like you are alone in your relationship? You were not created to be alone – especially in your marriage relationship. Do you know how to rekindle and enhance your relationship? We are here to give you a map that you can use to do this.

Would you like to change your heart in order to change the hearts of your children? We believe that most of life's hurts would be resolved early in life by implementing the ingredients found in *Changing Your Heart.* If you as parents knew that your children were going to be affected the way they are through divorce, would you knowingly bring such harm to them? To children, divorce is the same as parents placing them in a trauma unit, leaving them there and expecting them to figure out how to get well.

We are well aware of many situations that result in divorce, such as physical and mental abuse, drug addiction and alcoholism. Pornography and infidelity are on the rise at an alarming rate and wreak havoc on many relationships. But divorce is painful and life is not greener on the other side of the fence. So, if you could change your heart, what would it be worth to you?

Our goal is to help you repair your damaged heart. In turn, you will be able to heal the heart of your spouse.

Do you have a strained relationship with a co-worker, perhaps your boss? Changing your heart will help every relationship in your life. Changing your heart will give you the tools you need to create an atmosphere of trust, honesty and well-being. Not only will you attract harmony, peace and joy, your change of heart will enable you to give harmony, peace and joy to others. You will benefit from your changed heart in more ways than you can imagine.

Okay; we hear you saying, "Yeah, yeah, yeah. This isn't going to work for me." We know you might be apprehensive about believing that we can help you in your relationship. It's perfectly normal to have doubts. But you need to know that there's a method to our madness. We have helped couples for ten years, and we know these principles work to help mend relationships. We've worked with hundreds of couples at the brink of disaster, and they've reconciled by changing their hearts.

We can assure you with confidence that when you follow the map outlined in this book, you will experience a miraculous healing in your relationships. So we challenge you to plow forward and embrace these concepts, so that you can ultimately rekindle your relationships. You will experience joy, peace of mind and comfort as you share your life with your loved one.

Let's get right to it. We're going to share the ingredients up front in *Changing Your Heart*. We think it's awful when newscasters share an important bit of the news at one o'clock in the afternoon and then say, "Tune in at ten for the rest of the story." And we can't stand those books where the "solution" is hidden in the back of the book, forcing you to read the entire book before you get to the reason you bought it in the first place.

We want you to be uplifted from the beginning to the end of this book. Instead of probabilities, we want your mind to be open to the very real possibilities of change in every area of your life. We want you to see results in your life.

Based on what you're doing now, what's working and what isn't working in your relationship? We want your thinking to shift about yourself and about others. Are you ready to start revitalizing your life? It's going to take work. But it will only be hard if you make it hard.

ABOUT THE WORKSHEETS

The worksheets that follow each chapter are for you to use as you use the ingredients of *Changing Your Heart.*

These worksheets are designed for your use. If you are doing therapeutic letter writing, please keep them in your personal portfolio. For the most part, it is best that you do not mail them to your recipient. Use them again and again. Your change of heart is a lifelong process.

When you are enhancing, rekindling, restoring and repairing relationships, the best method is for you to meet personally and work on these issues together.

ACCOUNTABILITY PARTNER

You may want to find an **Accountability Partner**. Your Accountability Partner should be a trusted friend who will help you follow through in using the ingredients and help you with feedback on the change in your heart. Your Accountability Partner will know if you are doing your homework and will support you along the way. Write the name of your Accountability Partner below:

Accountability Partner:

_____

CHAPTER 1

Trouble

Do not let your hearts be troubled.
Trust in God, trust also in me. John 14:1

I t was late Friday afternoon. Michael's mind drifted off to the camping trip he and his family were leaving for later that evening. It had been a long and sad week for Michael, with the death of one of his co-workers, Alvin. It was good to let go of the trauma and instead embrace the excellent life Alvin had lived. He was a man of quiet strength; one Michael had admired so much that Alvin had become Michael's mentor as well as a good friend. Suzy, Alvin's wife, had come by a few hours earlier to collect his things and say goodbye to their staff. Alvin's shoes would be hard to fill.

 CB∞∞CCB∞

As Michael's mind drifted to think about the details of the upcoming trip, he thought, "Ah, the redwoods." He remembered the first time he touched a redwood as a young boy; the rough bark, the familiar musty smell that swarmed over him and the friendship he'd made with these massive partners so long ago. Being the oldest living entity on our planet, "This one was probably alive when Jesus was born," he'd thought all those years ago. The roots of a redwood intertwine with those of other giant redwoods, like a family, supporting the tall creatures with love and life-giving strength. Alone they cannot survive; together they weave a massive and strong forest. Oh, the stories the giant redwoods could tell.

Cঙওঔৎঙৎঙও

A knock on the door brought Michael back to the present. As he opened the door, he saw a young dark-haired man with sad eyes. Michael stuck out his hand for a hardy handshake. "Hi, I'm Michael Moore. You must be Tom." They shook hands for a long uncomfortable moment. Tom's handshake was weak, his palms clammy.

"Yes, I'm Tom," the dark-haired man responded.

"How can I help you?" Michael asked, although from their earlier phone conversation, Michael knew why Tom had come to his office.

"Well...My, ah, marriage is in trouble and someone told me you could help."

"Why don't you come in and sit down, Tom? This is a difficult topic for lots of men. You aren't the only one I've seen today. Can I offer you some coffee?"

Tom declined, almost sheepishly, already holding his head in his hands.

"First Tom, let me ask you some questions. Do you want the cream-and-sugar kind of help, which is fluff but no substance? Or do you want the kind of help that will most likely burn up some tiles on reentry, like the Space Shuttle? This means that there will be change involved. Change is never easy and it may be painful, at least at first."

Then Michael adjusted himself in his chair and waited patiently for an answer. When no audible answer came he added, "Honestly, I have never seen the cream-and-sugar approach work for anyone. So if that's the type of help you want, you'd probably do better with someone else. I am committed to helping you win."

With that, Tom's demeanor changed. He sat up straighter in his chair, leaned slightly forward and looked intensely into Michael's eyes with the fierce determination of a well-trained Shepherd playing catch in the backyard. At that moment, Tom decided that he wanted help and firmly replied, "Will you help me?"

And so they started. Tom told Michael the story of his seven-year marriage to Sonja. It had a rocky start, with hills, valleys, torrential downpours and very little joy. All this was accompanied by verbal abuse and yelling at their six-year-old daughter, Lisa. Tom had been laid off once, adding financial stress, doubt and insecurity to an already tough situation.

"Tom, you need to know that this is not about getting your wife back," Michael told him in a soft and deliberate voice.

Tom intently crossed his arms, pursed his lips and said, "Then what am I doing here?" His body language alone revealed the intense anger bubbling up behind the defiant attitude projected to the public.

"Tom, I am going to help you create the best possible conditions so your wife will choose to come back and restore your relationship," Michael replied. "It's sort of like growing a plant. Can you *make* the plant grow?"

"Not really," answered Tom.

"Well, what can you do?"

"I can prepare the soil by weeding it, tilling it and adding fertilizer and water."

Michael continued, "Very good. Only the powers of nature, God or whatever you want to call it can make the plant grow. So essentially, you create the best possible conditions for the plant to grow. Then, with consistency, persistence and the right combination of ingredients in the right amounts, you can achieve the desired result. A healthy..."

"Plant? Or are you talking about relationships?" Tom interrupted.

Michael just sat back and smiled. "What will you do to heal your marriage?" he asked.

"Anything," Tom answered.

"Anything?" Michael repeated.

"Yes, anything," came the reply. The air was thick as the word "anything" hung in the air between the two men. It was a word of desperation from a man at the end of his rope.

Then, in a soft voice, perhaps not even meaning to say it out loud, Michael said, "Why do people do what they do? Philosophers have struggled for centuries to find an answer to this question. What seems to be the answer is simple: People do what they do because of a perceived benefit."

To help illustrate his point, Michael said, "Let's say a friend offers you ten dollars to cross fifty feet on a two-by-four board between two ten-story buildings. Would you cross?"

"No way," Tom said.

"So there isn't enough perceived benefit to cross between buildings."

"That is correct."

Then Michael changed his challenge. "Now let's say your daughter is in the other building and the building is on fire. Would you cross that two-by-four to save your daughter?"

"I wouldn't give it a second thought. I would cross without hesitation."

"So," Michael continued, "What's different? It's the same board."

"The difference is that my daughter is in danger! So of course I would cross the two-by-four to save her."

"But why?"

"She's important to me. I would do anything; I would risk my life to save her."

"Then the perceived benefit of saving your daughter outweighs any danger of crossing a two-by-four between two ten-story buildings."

Without hesitating, Michael continued, his voice stronger, "Are you committed to restoring your marriage?" Before Tom could answer, he fired off a few more questions, not giving Michael time to rationalize his way out. "How will I know you are committed? Better yet, how will *Sonja know* you are committed? I am committed to helping you, Tom, but I will *not* do the work for you. And this *will* take work."

Tom felt the full weight of what Michael said, knowing that he needed to step up to the plate and accept the changes that would have to take place if his relationship was going to work. Wanting to fix it and actually doing something about it were two different things.

It all came down to the question that ripped deep into his heart. *Do I want to change my thoughts, my actions – my life – so that I will be able to survive even if Sonya doesn't want to come back?*

Tom felt he might pass out under the pressure he felt as his mind whirled with old thoughts of running away and starting over. *That can only be the enemy of my soul*, he thought.

He remembered the words from his youth and they flooded him like torrential waves. He knew the deep faith he had relied on time and time again. He knew his enemy was the devil. Tears welled in his eyes as he felt the warmth of God's Spirit upon him. He had not allowed himself to connect with God in a long time. The thoughts of evil left him as he realized where the thoughts were coming from.

Tom collected himself under the discerning stare of the other man. He didn't know what to do or say, but he knew his face said it all. Determined to fight his thoughts, Tom blurted out, "I'm ready for a challenge. I am ready to win her back."

And so it began.

CʒಔೞಌᏟʒಔ

A spectacular evening lightning storm lit the evening sky. The colors were intense in their story-telling with bright hues of blue, white and red. As Michael hurried home to finish packing for their family adventure to the redwoods, he couldn't help but ponder the last few words he'd said to Tom. "Are you a warrior? Are you a champion?"

He thought about the difficulties he and his wife, Maria, had experienced earlier in their marriage. He knew that he was himself a champion and he knew what it took to get there. He was excited about helping and he would go the distance with Tom. He would take another man on the quest to be all that God had intended him to be.

Later that evening, Michael finished loading the family mini-van. The air was charged with excitement and joy as they began their journey north for their campsite. With everyone safely buckled in, Maria sang with their daughters as they navigated the dark highway to their destination. Soon their twin seven-year-olds were asleep, no doubt dreaming peacefully about the adventures to come.

"You, okay honey?" Maria asked as she rubbed Michael's neck.

"Yeah. I'm just glad to be on this trip. It's come at the right time. God so loves me that He would have us leave today."

Maria talked excitedly about the redwoods. "Did you know that the redwoods are a lot like people?" she said. She continued her melodic chant. "You know, you hardly ever see a redwood standing alone in a forest. They don't make it on their own very well."

There was a long pause. "Michael, remember that God created me to take away your loneliness," she said softly. "He didn't want you to be alone. Most trees have root systems that are almost as deep as the trees are tall. You have a family to lean on when you feel the stress of this world pouring over the edges of your plate. I am here for you. I love you, Michael."

She continued with the history lesson happily as if it were a song. "And most trees usually have roots spread out only as wide as the branches. That is why redwoods are so unique. A 300-foot giant may have a root system only ten feet deep. Their roots may be hundreds of feet wide, intermingling with several other trees. They need each other to be strong and survive. Redwoods absorb their food through their branches, leaves and bark, because the root system isn't deep enough to provide the all nutrition they need. So you find redwood forests in places where there is an abundance of moisture in the air – like fog." Maria laughed because she knew she was rambling on to an audience of one.

As Michael slowed the mini-van, he turned on the wipers to wipe away a mist that had formed on the windshield. *Yep,* he thought, *fog should be right around the next bend.*

Sure enough, there it was, in the oncoming lights of the cars ahead. He thought of the redwoods and their relation to people. *We need each other,* Michael thought, *just like the redwoods need other redwoods.*

CRESORICARESO

"We need each other." Michael had told Tom earlier that day.

"We need each other?" Tom questioned as Michael walked around the room. There was a long pause as the question hung in the air.

"We...need... each... other?" Tom slowly asked again. To help clarify his wandering thoughts, Michael asked, "What do you do for a living?"

"I sell real estate," Tom answered.

"And do you do that by yourself?"

"Of course," Tom answered proudly. "I'm a self-made man." Then his voice trailed off, as he thought of Jenny, who took care of the paperwork, and Samantha, whose business sense had built their client base. She had mentored Tom for years.

Michael saw the change come over Tom's face. "Yeah; you're right," said Tom, thinking about the question truthfully. "We all need each other."

Michael forged on. "Before we discuss needs, let's discuss relationships. Let's pretend you have an identical twin brother named Tim."

"Okay."

"Let's say your father gave each of you a gift, an automobile. They were the same make and model, brand-new off the lot. You owned them for seven years. Now, you took excellent care of your vehicle – washed and polished it regularly, oil changes, tire rotations, new wiper blades when needed. You kept up with regular maintenance and upkeep. You were diligent in your task of keeping up with the car, recalls and things like that.

How would you answer if your father asked, 'Tom, what kind of gift did you receive?'"

"I would say it was great!"

Michael pressed on. "What would you have to do to keep the vehicle running?"

"Same things I had been doing."

"That's right. Now, on the other hand, your brother Tim didn't take care of his car at all. He didn't change the oil, or keep up with the tires or the wiper blades or tune-ups. Your father asked Tim the same question he asked you. 'What kind of gift did you receive, Tim?' What do you think your brother's answer would be, Tom?"

"Well, I suppose Tim would say he got a junker."

"Which one of you would be right?"

Tom answered, "Depending on the point of view, each of us could both be right."

"And you are both right, because..."

"Each of us made a choice. I chose to care for my gift, my imagery brother Tim did not."

"And which of the two vehicles would require the most resources to keep it running properly over time?"

"Tim's car would, of course."

Michael felt Tom was ready for more. "Tom, I'm going to go over some ingredients to help you create the best possible conditions for your wife to choose to restore your relationship." Michael used his fingers, touching each one as he counted off each concept. They are:

1. **Stepping into integrity**, which means being honest, reliable and truthful at all times, not just when it's convenient or when others are looking.

2. **Forgiving others**, which simply means to stop resenting or being angry with others for what they've done (or haven't done) to you.

3. **Asking others for forgiveness** for things you have (or haven't) done, knowingly or unknowingly, to hurt someone else.

4. **Investing your time** in people.

5. **Supporting the relational needs of others** by discussing what their needs are and meeting those needs without necessarily having your own needs met.

6. **Bless with your tongue**, which means speaking words of affirmation and hope into others lives.

Applying all of these ingredients with a changed heart will result in the restoration of relationships."

Michael paused, then said, "Tell me about the ingredients you'd need if you were baking a cake."

Tom answered, "Well, you've got flour, milk, eggs, butter, sugar and salt."

"If you mixed them in the right proportions, do you have a cake?"

"No," Tom replied.

"What do you think still needs to happen in order for the cake to be done?"

"Well, you have to put the ingredients in a pan, then into the oven and bake them at the correct temperature."

"Correct. So the key to baking a cake is the correct amount of heat for the correct amount of time. Would you agree?"

"Sure."

"If you don't add heat to your ingredients or if you left out a critical ingredient, what would happen?"

"If you don't add heat, you'd have a runny mess." If you leave out an ingredient, like I did once, you might end up with a science project," Tom chuckled.

"Right you are. Could you add other ingredients to your cake mix to enhance the flavor, say some vanilla or cinnamon?"

"Yes, you could do that and the cake could be different."

"So the ingredients listed above aren't exclusive, but you must be careful when you add other ingredients. Once again, **Changing Your Heart** is the key.

21

"Let's talk about how to change your heart first. Then we'll talk about the other ingredients."

"That sounds good," Tom said, and Michael saw that a bit of hope had emerged.

CHAPTER 2

Changing Your Heart vs. Malicious Compliance

For as he thinks in his heart so is he. Prov 23:7
For out of the abundance of the heart the mouth speaks.
Matt 12:34b

"What does changing your heart mean?" Michael asked a rhetorical question. He said, "Actually, it's probably easier to define the *absence* of a changed heart. We know that cold is the absence of heat and darkness is the absence of light. Well, a lack of love in your heart is the absence of a change of heart."

"Okay, go ahead."

"Have you ever met someone who was maliciously compliant?" Without taking a breath, Michael forged ahead. "I'm paraphrasing the dictionary a bit, but malicious is defined as: 'mean, the opposite of nice, extremely unpleasant.' And we'd define compliant as 'one who obeys the rules.' So when you put the two words together, you get someone who obeys the rules only because he has to. And unfortunately, that person is evilly delighted when obeying the rules because it causes chaos.

"People who have malicious compliance in their hearts will do only what they are told to do. They don't volunteer to help others. They want to do the minimum and receive the maximum. Maliciously compliant people will do something they know is wrong, just so they can point the finger at a manager or spouse and reply, 'You (or they) told me to do it.' Sound familiar, Tom?"

"Yeah, you nailed me. When I do a project at work, I comply but I don't put my heart into it. With Sonja, I help out around the house, but only half-heartedly."

"Did you notice that you framed each of those behaviors with a lack of heart – you 'don't put your *heart* into it' and you 'help out *half-heartedly*' when you work around the house?"

Tom almost smiled, "Well, how about that? I guess I did."

"Well, changing your heart is exactly opposite. You've heard phrases like, 'He plays with a lot of heart.'

You can feel it. It means you help others because you *want* to do it. You want to do the right thing for the right reason.

"Changing your heart is about establishing relationships, not so you can *get* something; but because relationships are the essence of human existence that never goes away.

"Have you ever heard of the classic tale, *A Christmas Carol?*"

Tom responded "Sure, who hasn't? We watch the movie at Christmas every year."

"Then you know that Ebenezer Scrooge embodies the concept of changing your heart," Michael said. "Scrooge is maliciously compliant. He is mean-spirited and lonely throughout the tale. Three spirits visit him in an attempt to get him to change. Why didn't the visit from the Spirit of Christmas Past succeed? It's simple, really. Scrooge didn't have a change of heart. Same with the Spirit of Christmas Present. Scrooge's heart did not change. Finally! The third time was the charm; Scrooge had a change of heart after the third visit.

"Oh, what joy! He chose to live with integrity; he stopped being greedy. Scrooge chose to forgive others and he asked for forgiveness of his own. He supported the physical and relational needs of others and out of his mouth came blessings for others. It's a true picture of changing your heart and using the ingredients that repair relationships!"

"I agree that this is a good picture, but it's just a story," Tom pointed out.

"Okay," Michael said. "Let me tell you some stories about real people who lived on our planet."

The first story is about a man who didn't have a change of heart. In his day, he was one of the wealthiest men on earth. He was an aviator, a film producer and director and a philanthropist. He set world airspeed records and built the famous Spruce Goose airplane.

"He's famous, not just for what he did in his professional life, but for his eccentric behavior later in life. When he died, his appearance had changed so much, they had to use his fingerprints to identify him. On his deathbed, you can bet that this man didn't long for more money, or more airplanes or more property; not anything physical. On his deathbed, Howard Hughes longed for more and deeper relationships with other people. How sad.

"This next story is about a woman who exemplifies someone with a changed heart. She was born into poverty, but she saw others who were even worse off than she was. This Roman Catholic nun founded the Missionaries of Charity in Calcutta, India. She ministered to the poor, sick, orphaned and dying for more than forty years and watched her mission spread around the world.

"By the 1970s, she was famous for her work with the poor and needy. She won the Nobel Peace Prize for her humanitarian work. After she died, Pope John Paul II gave her the title Blessed Teresa of Calcutta.

"Mother Theresa dedicated her life to building relationships and changing the lives of thousands. And when she died, millions around the world mourned."

Tom was mesmerized. "So a truly changed heart means giving all you've got."

"That's right. What was the common thread of those stories?" asked Michael.

Tom thought for a moment, "I suppose in *A Christmas Carol*, it's easy to see the change of heart in Scrooge. In the case of Howard Hughes, he had lots of *stuff*, but his heart wasn't connected to anyone else's heart. Mother Teresa devoted her life to connecting her heart to other people's hearts."

Michael moved on, "You're right. Like I said, it is hard to define, but you'll know it when you see. It's the same as being in love, you know when you're in love and when you're not."

Michael stood and crossed the room, where he reached into the refrigerator and pulled out two bottles of water. As he walked back across the room, and extended his arm to give a bottle of water to Tom, he said, "I've met people in their fifties, sixties and seventies who will not change their hearts. They choose to stay where they are. People like this usually have a bitter attitude towards everything. These people talk about their dogs, neighbors, spouses, friends and you never hear anything positive about anything.

"It's very uncomfortable to be around these people for any length of time. They would rather blame others for their circumstances than actually do the changing themselves. It's always somebody else's fault. They can never say, 'I did it.' Imagine what their relationships would look like if they would just surrender their hearts? For these people, changing their hearts would allow them to meet the needs of everyone around them, instead of expecting everyone else to meet their needs.

"It always starts deep inside. There's a joy that everyone can have, but we have to choose to want it more than anything else."

"Tom," Michael asked, "Do you expect things from your wife that she can't seem to deliver or do the way you want her to?"

Tom was visibly moved by Michael's question. He welled up with tears and answered slowly, his voice at the point of breaking, "Michael, I do have high expectations and I know I have pressured Sonja to meet them."

Michael gently placed his hand on Tom's forearm and said, "My friend, you have gone through half the battle. Just acknowledging that you've been wrong shows that your heart is ready for a change.

"Let's move further back in time. Two thousand years ago, a Jewish Man demonstrated the importance of changing your heart. He traveled extensively with twelve men that he hand-picked to be at his side.

Just imagine the personalities each of these disciples displayed. John, one of the disciples, refers to himself as the disciple who Jesus loved. Then we have Peter, who was very impetuous during a storm, stepped out of a boat and walked towards Jesus. Jesus knew each of his disciples intimately. He loved John, and He loved the adventurous and daring Peter. Jesus is just as interested in us, too.

Isn't it interesting that Jesus chose to build relationships with his disciples for the last three years of his life? I'm sure He could have completed God's purpose of redemption without building relationships. In fact, those who were closest to Jesus during his trial and crucifixion fled during his time of greatest need.

"So why did he bother to build relationships? It could be because Jesus wanted his disciples to experience a changed heart for themselves. Then He sent them out into the world to show others how to change their hearts, too. Here's an amazing thing, though: One of the twelve disciples didn't experience a change of heart. Even though Jesus had hand-picked Judas and spent three years with him, Judas betrayed him in the end.

"Tom," Michael said, "I believe you have chosen to change your heart and I know that changing your heart is the key. You are the only one who can choose to change. If your intention is to restore your marriage, then that will be your result."

ೞೲಐೱೞೲ

Through the fog, Michael barely saw their destination. Maria seemed overjoyed to be there. Their two little angels were slumped over, ears touching their shoulders, certainly dreaming about the next day's adventures. The headlamps beamed into the campground, diffused by the fog. It was almost like a scene from a Christmas story, fairy tale-like.

Michael sighed with relief. His body ached a bit from the long drive, but he was glad they had arrived safely. With as much care as they could, the couple quietly made camp. They set up the tent, inflated the mattresses, shook out the sleeping bags and lit the lanterns. It had become a well-choreographed dance between them. They had camped many times before and each knew instinctively what to do.

Finally, their camp was ready. Michael and Maria gently transported their greatest treasure, the twins, and tucked them quietly and snugly in their sleeping bags. They were careful to close the windows in the car so animals would not eat their food. They turned the lights off in the car, flicked on their flashlights, smiling like two giddy children in the misty night.

Satisfied, they turned in for the night. Shucking her shoes, Maria reached out to touch her hand on her husband's shoulder. She whispered, "You, my love, have a great heart. And I love that so much about you." Michael remembered his conversation with Tom, and almost chuckled to himself, *Yeah changing your heart.*

CRESTOREORCORESTO

Changing Your Heart

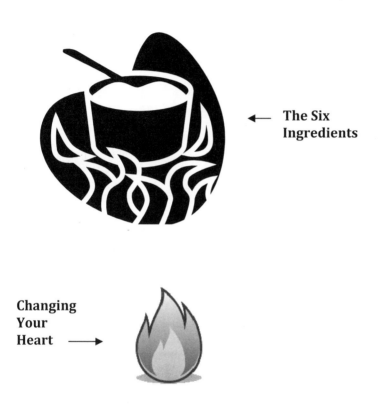

← **The Six Ingredients**

Changing Your Heart ⟶

Changing Your Heart is the Heat That Allows the Other Ingredients to be Effective.

CHAPTER 3

Stepping Into Integrity

May integrity and uprightness protect me,
because my hope is in You. Psalms 25:21

T om replied, "Changing my heart; that sounds simple enough. What's next?"

Michael wondered if Tom really understood, but he decided to move forward. He introduced *Stepping into Integrity.*

"There's not really a *next* ingredient per se, Tom, because each of the ingredients is equally important. But the first ingredient we'll talk about is called *Stepping into Integrity.* It means being honest, reliable and truthful."

"I like the sound of that," Tom said. "It's like moving forward."

Michael nodded in agreement. "Right. Now, the principle of integrity is very simple. But sometimes people make it difficult. You build relationships through integrity – it's that simple. It's kind of like the foundation of a house. A house that's built on a poor foundation will eventually have some sort of problems. (See Matt 7:24)

Do you remember the story of the three pigs? Adding poorly made walls to a poor foundation will definitely get your house blown down by the big bad wolf! Something small happens, and it's like a tornado has hit. Then you add a little fire and boy oh boy, sometimes there's not enough water to put it out."

"So if integrity is defined as being truthful or trustworthy then any relationship without trust will be in jeopardy. And by standing in integrity and keeping your word, you'll build trust. That's a mouthful but I get it," Tom said.

"How long does it take to build trust?" Michael asked, not fully convinced that Tom understood the concept yet.

Tom thought for a moment and said, "I suppose it depends on the person."

"What else?" Michael pressed him.

Tom replied with confidence, "I think it also depends on how much a person has been hurt before, how dependable you have been with that person and how willing you are to be open and honest."

Michael was pleased. He smiled warmly. "It's more than that. How about this – Do you cheat on your taxes?"

Tom blushed, "Everybody does that, right?"

"If a person cheats on his taxes, then he has stepped out of integrity. Even if the perception is that everyone cheats on taxes."

Michael continued. "Integrity is more than saying or doing the right things; it is who you are as a person – even when no one is looking."

"Who I am, as a person?" Tom questioned Michael's response.

"Tom, let me use a personal story to emphasize this point. One of my female cousins has a mission in life to 'clean up' our world. You know, stop greenhouse gases, repair the ozone layer, stop pollution, save the rain forest and things like that. All are noble and honorable goals for her mission.

"Well, one day our family went to a movie. After the movie, I asked my cousin what she'd done with her empty candy wrappers, popcorn bucket and drink cup. You've probably guessed that she left them in the theater on the floor near her seat. So then I asked her how that fit in with her mission to clean up the world. She said, 'Oh, Michael, that doesn't count in the movie theater!' What more can I say? If my cousin's true intention is to clean up our planet, then her integrity wouldn't have allowed her to leave trash in a theater – or anywhere, for that matter.

"So...If you don't *live* in integrity – if you look at pornography, abuse alcohol or drugs, lie, cheat, have sex outside your marriage, are addicted to work, the Internet, TV – the list is practically endless. If this is your life, then *stop* and **Step Into Integrity.** It is the key ingredient for building trust in all relationships."

☙❧☙❧☜☙❧

That night, Michael drifted off to sleep, knowing his family was safe and secure in their tent. In his dreams, the redwoods came alive. The mighty redwoods are a wonderful example of integrity. They just aren't trees; they are resistant to bugs, infections, rot and natural disasters. Still, they're just trees being trees.

In his dreams, Michael flew between them, around and over them. He visualized Alvin, his recently departed friend. Alvin and his wife Suzy were people of great integrity. They were conscious about saying what they meant and meaning what they said.

In his dream, Michael went back to the night when Michael and Maria's twins were born. He flew to the 'Hospital of the Redwood,' where Maria gave birth. The girls had arrived a month early, their premature bodies still developing. The newborns needed a lot of care. Incubators kept them warm and monitored their vital signs and nurses provided nutrition and personal care.

Right beside them were Alvin and Suzy, people of incredible integrity. Alvin said, "Michael, you take care of your family. Suzy and I will take care of your home and business." Knowing they could depend on Alvin and Suzy, Michael and Maria spent important hours at the hospital caring for their newborn babies, while Alvin and Suzy orchestrated meals, laundry, yard work and so much more. It's as though a small pair of redwood seeds took root and began their journey through life just as those tiny babies did on that night.

In his dream, Michael planted a redwood sapling in memory of a man of integrity, his friend Alvin. As he did, he said, "Oh you tiny sapling, you will grow in a mighty tree, a symbol of the strength of my friend Alvin."

છ૪ણ૪ળ૪૪

The Ingredient of Stepping Into Integrity

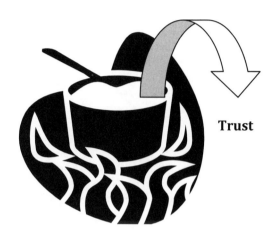

Trust

The Ingredient of **Stepping Into Integrity**
Allows you to Build and Manifest Trust.

Stepping Into Integrity Worksheet

Truthfulness

Obey the Law

Sexual Morality

Keeping Your Word

Honesty

Uprightness

Reliability

Honor

Thinking of Others First

Moderation of Life Activities; Such as TV, Alcohol, Sports, Work

List the characteristic(s) of integrity you are stepping into now and in the future:

_____

_____

_____

_____

_____

_____

_____

_____

Stepping Into Integrity Worksheet

Write a plan to display the characteristic(s):

_____

_____

_____

_____

_____

_____

_____

_____

_____

_____

_____

_____

_____

_____

_____

_____

_____

_____

_____

_____

CHAPTER 4

Forgiving Others

Do not judge, and you will not be judged.
Do not condemn, and you will not be condemned.
Forgive, and you will be forgiven. Luke 6:37

"Have you ever been to a redwood forest?" asked Michael. Tom shook his head no. "You can learn a lot of life lessons from the forest," Michael offered. "For instance, a redwood that's experienced some trauma is more useful than a tree that hasn't experienced trauma."

"What do you mean?" Tom asked.

Michael continued, "Let's say a fire has burned out a portion of a tree near the ground. That tree is so big that the burned-out area serves as a mini-cave. Early settlers used that area to keep livestock penned up for protection during a storm. So you see; a 'damaged' redwood could be more useful than a healthy tree."

"So this trauma I'm going through could be used for good?" Tom's statement trailed off into a question.

"It is certainly a possibility," Michael replied.

As the questions continued back and forth, the men began to relax in each other's company.

"Don't you think that cancer survivors are some of the best people for encouraging people who have just found out they have cancer?"

"They sure are," Tom answered. "So are you saying it might be possible for me to help someone else?"

"Absolutely," Michael said. "Now let's get back to our redwood friend. When that redwood was on fire, what did it need most?"

"Someone or something to put out the fire," Tom said.

"That's right. But what else did the redwood need?" Michael continued his inquiry.

Tom leaned forward and speculated. "Hmm. I suppose it needed time to heal."

Michael clapped, "Yes – It needed someone to guide or guard it until the damaged area healed. Then what?"

Tom felt secure in his answers to Michael's questions. He realized that he actually knew the solution. He answered with confidence, "Now the damaged area on the redwood could be used for another purpose."

"There you go," was Michael's relieved response.

Before Michael could add another word, Tom continued, with a little grin, "Then what? I could use those illustrations in my life. In other words, I need to seek healing and then wait until I can help someone else."

"Hmmm," Michael hummed.

Tom chuckled, "Yeah, I got it." He felt the full weight of his own thoughts on his shoulders.

"How do I mend the trauma that I have caused in my relationship with my wife? Michael," he said, almost under his breath, "How do I mend the trauma that I have caused others?" The reality was sobering and somber for Tom. He moved uneasily in this chair, shifting his weight from side to side.

Michael broke the tension gently by saying, "Tom, do you remember the cake ingredients we talked about earlier? We're going to use those ingredients to change your heart and I know you will see a shift.

"Forgiveness, forgiveness, forgiveness is the key ingredient for healing," Michael continued.

"Tom, Jesus was one of the most gifted speakers of all time. Have you heard of the Sermon on the Mount?"

Tom looked puzzled and said, "I'm not sure. Why what does it say?

"Jesus taught us how to forgive others," Michael replied. "Do you mind if I read some of it to you?" Michael said as he flipped through his Bible.

"No not at all," Tom replied. He felt uncomfortable because he hadn't been reading the Bible he had been given so long ago.

"Ah, here it is," Michael said. "Jesus said, 'For if you forgive men when they sin against you, your heavenly Father will also forgive you. But if you do not forgive men their sins, your Father will not forgive your sins.' (Matthew 6: 14-15)

"So according to that passage, it is clearly in *our* best interest to forgive others. Forgiveness is not the same as trust, though. You can only gain trust by being trustworthy over time. Sometimes it takes a long time to rebuild trust. It doesn't happen overnight.

"Forgiveness is not being a wimp," Michael continued. "It is not allowing people to walk all over you. We aren't doormats, nor should we be treated as doormats.

"Forgiveness is not a permission slip to repeat sinful behavior at a future date. In other words, once you ask someone to forgive you, don't purposely repeat that behavior.

"Forgiveness is the act of letting go of an offense. When you detect an offense or you resent someone, a lot of time you perceive that it happened. It might not have happened the way you thought it did.

"Sometimes we carry things around and other people have no idea that they have even done anything to us. So you go around resenting someone else; you let it rule your life and your actions and the other person never even knows it happened.

"Let go of the offense and resentful feelings you have towards others and do not pick it up again."

"I'm not sure what you mean," Tom said honestly.

Michael asked, "Other than Sonja, has anyone offended you?"

"Of course."

"What happened?" Michael asked.

Tom dropped his eyes toward the floor. "Well, three years ago, my jerk brother-in-law from Croatia made some rude comments at the dinner table during one of our Christmas parties. I was really offended and felt the comments were directed at me. Man, I let him have it. I told him the comments he made were not appreciated in my house, but not in such nice words. I put a stop to that nonsense right there." Tom paused, saddened.

"So tell me, Tom," Michael said. "What was the outcome of this behavior? Do you think the outcome was fair?"

"He and his family haven't been to our home since that day," Tom said. "And my bull-headedness in this situation has caused unnecessary tension between me and my wife." Tom sighed and continued. "Do I think it's fair for them not to visit us? Actually, I think it's a little on the extreme side."

"Would you like to provide an opportunity for healing in this situation?" Michael asked.

"I guess so."

Michael was firm. "The answer is either yes or no. There's no guessing here."

"It wasn't even my fault." Tom paused, mulling the answer over. He didn't want to give in to his anger, but after a few moments and remembering the pain his actions had caused his wife and himself, he said, "Yes."

"So here we go," Michael said.

Forgive Others

"I recommend you write it down on a piece of paper. Be specific about what happened or what you perceived happened. Here's a piece of paper. Go ahead and do it now." Michael handed Tom a piece of paper and a pen. "Go ahead, Tom. Write it down."

Tom wrote: *I was offended that my brother-in-law used crude language in my home during a Christmas party.*

"Now write that you forgive your brother-in-law."

"No way! He was wrong, not me!"

Michael gave Tom a questioning look. "Didn't you just agree that you wanted to provide an opportunity for healing with your brother-in-law?"

"Oh, okay, *okay!*"

"Remember, it's your heart we're changing here."

Tom wrote: *I forgive my brother-in-law for the crude language he used in my house during a Christmas party.*

"How do you feel?" Michael asked.

"I don't feel anything," Tom said. "Am I supposed to feel something?" Tom and Michael sat quietly for a few moments, long enough for Tom's words to reach his heart. Then he spoke. "Actually Michael, I feel relieved."

Michael was proud of the steps Tom had taken. He almost didn't want to say the next words. "Tom, we aren't done yet."

"What!?" was Tom's astonished response.

The Ingredient of Forgiving Others

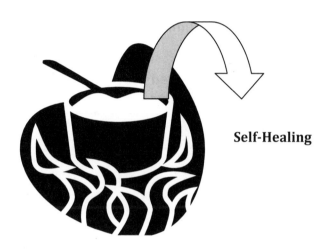

Self-Healing

The Ingredient of **Forgiving Others**
Brings about Self-Healing.

Forgiving Others Worksheet

Describe the offense (be specific):

_____

_____

_____

_____

_____

_____

_____

_____

Write down your forgiveness for the offender:

_____

_____

_____

_____

_____

_____

_____

_____

_____

CHAPTER 5

Asking Others for Forgiveness

Forgive us our sins, for we also forgive everyone
who sins against us Luke 11:4a

"You're kidding, right?" Tom said. His face felt flushed.

"No," Michael replied. "In order to complete this, you have to ask your brother-in-law to forgive you."

"Why?" Tom questioned, exasperated.

"Tom, didn't you say he hasn't been to your home since this happened?"

"Yeah," Tom said sheepishly.

"Why hasn't this family visited you in three years, Tom?" Michael said, almost yelling.

"I guess our relationship has cooled off." Tom would have given anything to have been in another room.

Michael didn't let up. "Do you think he could still be offended at what happened?"

"I suppose so."

Michael was about to hit a home run. "Do you think that asking him to forgive you could provide healing for his heart?"

"Sure, I guess it could," Tom said.

"Here's the mysterious thing about asking him to forgive you," Michael explained. "In doing so, you will become healed as well." Michael held his arms straight over his head, like a referee at a football game, "Touchdown!"

"Okay, I'll try," Tom replied.

Michael squinted and said, "How about making a commitment to ask him for forgiveness?"

Tom sat back, scratched his head and finally said, "I commit to asking my brother-in-law for forgiveness."

"By when?" Michael pressed him.

"By the end of the week."

"That means...by Saturday at midnight?"

"Yes, yes, yes!"

"Good."

CʒഔฦᏣʒഔ

The day passed quickly; Michael and his family laughed and enjoyed each other's company all day. They ended the day with a long hike. As they returned, Maria said, "Wow. They're getting heavy!"

"I guess we should have planned this a little better," said Michael, puffing as he carried Gina. Maria carried Tina, who was the lightest of the twins. "This hike was a little too long for them. But I wouldn't have traded it for anything."

That night, Gina and Tina were safely tucked in their sleeping bags. Maria yawned as she readied herself for sleep. Michael's flashlight panned the area. He wanted to make sure everything was as it should be before he got into his sleeping bag. The food was safely locked inside the mini-van, its windows tightly closed. "Don't want any animals getting into the food," he thought again. He turned off all the lights and lanterns, except the flashlight he carried. He could barely make out lights through the fog in the distance.

He was almost ready to enter the tent when something caught his eye. "I'll be there in a minute," he whispered to Maria. "Okay," she whispered back. He approached one of the nearby giant trees. "Wow. What happened to you, big fella?" Shining the light, he noticed a huge area in the middle of the tree that had been burned. It was so large that his entire family and their equipment could fit inside. As he touched the tree, he almost felt it answer, "I'm glad I survived. I am here to provide security for your family." Michael went into his tent, ready for sleep. His family softly slumbered. "Thank you, big fella. I do feel safe." And with that, Michael drifted off to sleep, too.

"Sometimes it takes time," Michael said. "Remember when we talked earlier about the redwood forest? Well, a redwood may take twenty years to grow to maturity, but it happens. Once again, this isn't about getting Sonja 'back.' It is about preparing the soil for the relationship to grow and providing the nutrients for your relationship to flourish. It's about removing weeds from the soil to keep the relationship from being choked.

"See, just as you can over-water or over-fertilize a plant, it's possible to overdo the ingredients in a relationship. You have to find a balance.

"All things in life rely on balance. In order to 'be,' the giant redwoods need a balance of air, moisture, sun, warmth and interdependence on the surrounding trees."

"To *be* what?" asked Tom.

"To be what they were intended to be – trees. And not just any trees, but trees of excellence," Michael added. "So just give it time."

The next week, Michael and Tom got together again. Tom was almost breathless. "I don't believe it!"

"What is it?" Michael was excited now, too. Tom's enthusiasm was infectious.

"Well," Tom started, "It worked! My brother-in-law and I, we are..." Tom was at a loss for words.

"Tell me about it," Michael urged.

"We had a family get-together last weekend. As I told you, my brother-in-law is from Croatia. So sometimes his accent can be thick. He calls me Tomm*iee!* Well, as you and I discussed, I approached him. I took his hands in mine and said, 'Andres, I want to do something with you.' He pulled his hands away and said, 'No Tomm*iee!*' I said, 'Please let me do this.' I really think he felt my heart had changed. I reached for his hands and looked into his eyes. Then I sincerely said, 'You were at my house for a Christmas party and I was rude to you.

Please forgive me.' He stared at me for a moment, then it seemed as though a cloud crossed over his face and he broke into a big toothy grin. He patted me on the back with enough force for me to expel all the breath in my lungs.

"While I was trying to catch my breath, he said, 'It's okay, Tomm*ie!*' The night was magical! We were friends again. We talked about doing things in the future, things like our families going fishing together. Wow! But the best was yet to come. Later in the week, Sonja talked on the phone to Irene, Andres' wife. Irene said that since Christmas, Andres didn't want to have anything to do with me ever again. He was really upset with me. Now Irene says it is alright and there is peace."

"Wow," said Michael. "That is, as the kids say, *gi-normous!* Congratulations, Tom. Well done."

"Michael, it was unbelievable. I wouldn't have believed it if I hadn't seen the healing between us with my own eyes."

"Way to go, dude!"

The two men did a high five. Their hands slapped with a loud clap, bringing satisfaction to them both.

ᏣᏍᏬᏍᏬᎧᏣᏍᏬ

The redwoods are incredible. Their longevity makes it seem that their growth is very slow. It seems as though nothing bothers them – not animals, not insects, not sickness, not lightning, not fire. It is as if they let everything go.

Like forgiveness!

ೞ೦೦೩೦೩ೞ೦

The Ingredient of
Asking Others for Forgiveness

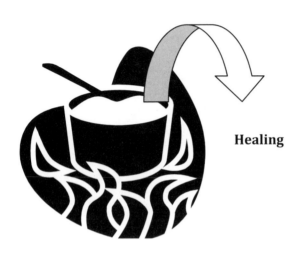

Healing

The Ingredient of **Asking Others for Forgiveness** allows Healing in the Hearts of Others

Asking Others for Forgiveness Worksheet

Ask the other person for forgiveness by stating how you hurt that person without justification (remember to be specific).

State your behavior was wrong.

Ask to be forgiven.

Write down your plan:

_____

_____

_____

_____

_____

_____

_____

_____

_____

_____

_____

_____

_____

CHAPTER 6

Time

You're blessed when you care. At the moment of being 'care-ful'
you'll find yourselves cared for. Matt 5:7

T ime is elusive. At 'times,' you seem to have plenty
of it. At other 'times,' it seems to be running out.
That's how Tom felt. Time was running out on his
relationship with his wife. He met with Michael to
discuss the ingredient of time.

The men shook hands before they sat down to begin.

"How are you, Tom?"

"I'm okay. I'll admit that I'm really curious about this
ingredient called time."

Michael paused. "Time," he said. It was as if he was
saying hello to an old and treasured friend. "We have
only so much and we don't know how much we have."

Michael paused to allow Tom to grasp the point about how precious time is to everyone.

Tom seemed antsy. "Come on, come on already. Let's get a move on."

Michael sensed Tom's impatience. He paused even longer.

Tom drummed his fingers. He sighed, time dragged.

Michael finally spoke, "What did you just learn?"

Tom laughed cynically. "Why, nothing!"

"Nothing?" Michael queried.

Tom's thoughts screamed from deep inside his being. *Why am I so impatient?* "I suppose I expected us to get right to it. You know, to discuss time. But you made me wait."

"Oh," Michael said slowly and deliberately. "I made you wait?"

"You didn't say anything, so I had to wait," Tom said.

"Tom, you had the choice to leave if you wanted to."

"I guess you're right."

"There's a term called 'quality time' that people talk about"

"Yeah, I say that myself," Tom said. "I'll say I've spent quality time with my daughter."

"Does she say 'Oh, Dad thank you for the quality time?'"

"No, she just says she had a great time with her dad!" Tom chuckled, "It tickles me to hear her laugh with such pure joy."

"So the essence of being with her is called time."

"Yes. That's right."

"Tom, are you sure your daughter doesn't say *quality time*?"

"I'm sure."

"That's right. The concept of this ingredient is investing and spending time with someone."

Suddenly Michael changed subjects. "Did you date Sonja before you were married?"

The question caught Tom off guard. "Yes, I did."

"Do you date your wife now?"

"Date my wife? Heck no! She's my wife. We do stuff together, like watch our daughter in school plays and such. But date Sonja? No."

"But you dated her before?"

"Yes, before we were married, we went out all the time."

"What was that like?"

"We went water skiing, she's pretty good. We hiked together, oh and I enjoyed the time we stayed at a hotel in Reno. We went to some shows."

Tom relaxed as he thought about the adventures he and his wife had together. He thought for a minute. "I didn't realize how long it has been..." Tom's voice became a whisper.

"What can you do differently?"

"I can date my wife."

"Excellent. How about some guidelines for dating? Maria and I call ours date night, although that's not very original"

"Date night, cool. That's easy enough."

"On our date nights, we use the following guidelines:

- The date must be something you both enjoy.
- You must be alone, just the two of you. No double dating, no kids, no parents, no one else – just the two of you.
- No talking about money.
- No talking about kids.
- No talking about either of your families.
- No talking about anything negative.
- The date must be a minimum of 30 minutes."

"Michael, holy smokes; it sounds as though you can't talk about anything."

Michael laughed and said, "Of course you can. You can discuss your hopes and dreams for the future. Discuss the reason you were attracted to each other in the first place. Enjoy each other's company. You know how to date; you told me you dated before you were married. Let's make a list of some activities that you and Sonja enjoy."

Tom wrote his list, smiling as he wrote each item.

When Tom finished his list, Michael continued. "Another way time can be an ingredient is when you devote time in the form of a marriage meeting."

"A marriage meeting?"

"A marriage meeting, along with date night, should be a habit for you. The two of you would be wise to schedule a date and marriage meeting on a regular basis."

"What the heck is a marriage meeting?"

Michael said, "I thought you'd never ask."

Then Michael explained the ingredient of time and marriage meetings.

A marriage meeting looks like this:

- Schedule a time when you each have **time** to devote to the meeting.
- Make an agenda.
- Eliminate distractions.
- Discuss financial issues.
- Discuss parenting issues.
- Discuss and coordinate schedules.
- Discuss future plans.
- Stick to the agenda.

With that, the men wrapped up their discussion. "The whole purpose of a marriage meeting, Tom, is to keep you connected with your mate on every level.

"It is a tool to practice, slowing yourself down long enough to open up and be vulnerable with each other. Keep the atmosphere positive and uplifting during your marriage meetings. Make it a time to safely share issues. Communicate, communicate, and communicate!"

Tom began slowly, "Michael, I'm not used to this 'vulnerable' sharing as you called it. Do I have to show all of my emotions and open up? I just don't think I can do this. Sonja is always harping on me that I don't talk to her. Well, I *do* talk to her."

"When you talk to Sonja, from your point of view, Tom, what kinds of things do *you* talk about?"

Tom answered, "I talk about my day at work, my co-workers, how our daughter is doing, you know, that kind of stuff. But nothing fluffy."

"So what you're saying is everything else that you could share would make you uncomfortable and perhaps be *fluffy* as you put it," Michael said. "Tom, this is just a platform for you to start communicating with your wife, for you to really be with her on a one to one basis. She loves you and really wants to get to know you. I believe that you feel the same way about her, but you don't know how to go about it. Can you trust me and trust yourself to believe that it isn't going to be as hard as you think?

Tom finally spoke. "Okay, I'll give it a try. I will follow the plan, even though I feel a little skeptical and apprehensive about the whole thing. Thank you, Michael for taking the time to walk me through this, I really appreciate your willingness to help me."

Both men stood, shook hands and left each other feeling very good and encouraged. Tom even felt that time was finally on his side.

CR෴೮෴೮෴

Without a word or sound of any kind, the serenity of the massive nearby giants seemed to watch over Michael's family. Such peace, he thought. Maria was just rising, and he basked in the tranquility of the moment. The first rays of the sun pierced the forest canopy. The warm steam from his coffee did a dance in and out and around the light rays.

I will take my own advice, he thought, pouring Maria a cup of hot coffee. She glided toward him. Quietly, so as not to wake the children, she embraced the cup and gave him a kiss on the cheek. "Husband of love," she said. He never tired of that nickname; it sounded so sweet and tasted like honey on his lips.

I will take my own advice. I will bless with my tongue, Michael thought. "My dearest, I bless you today with abundance in all areas, with a strong and healthy body, with peace and joy, with passion for your purpose." As a tear welled in the corner of her eyes, she melted into his arms. Their embrace lasted a long time. That is what the redwoods have, and what they foster in others – time.

CBℂℂCB

The Ingredient of Time

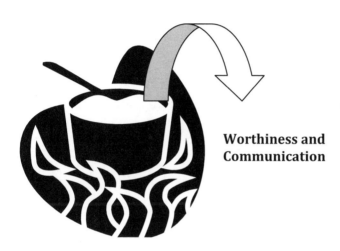

Worthiness and Communication

The Ingredient of **Time**

Brings about a Feeling of Worthiness in Others and Communication in Relationships

Time Worksheet

Date each other regularly.

Date Night Guidelines:

- The date must be something you both enjoy.
- You must be alone, just the two of you. No double dating, no kids, no parents, no one else – just the two of you.
- No talking about money.
- No talking about kids.
- No talking about either of your families.
- No talking about anything negative.
- The date must be a minimum of 30 minutes.
- Discuss what attracted you to each other.
- Discuss your goals and dreams for the future.

Time Worksheet

Date Night

Write down the activities you and your mate enjoy doing together. Write down the date of your date night.

Activity   Date

_____

_____

_____

_____

_____

_____

_____

_____

_____

_____

_____

_____

_____

_____

_____

_____

Time Worksheet

Marriage Meeting
Schedule a marriage meeting on a regular basis.

- Schedule a time when both partners have time to devote to the meeting.
- Make an agenda
- Eliminate distractions (phones, children sleeping or playing elsewhere, etc.)
- Discuss financial issues.
- Discuss parenting issues.
- Discuss and coordinate schedules.
- Discuss the future.
- Stick to your agenda.

Time Worksheet

Marriage Meeting

Agenda

Financial Issues

_____

_____

Parenting Issues

_____

_____

Schedules

_____

_____

Future Plans

_____

_____

Open Forum

CHAPTER 7

Supporting the Relational Needs of Others

Carry each other burdens Gal 6:2a

"You're good for nothing!" Sonja yelled.

"Why are you doing this?" Tom yelled back.

They had been arguing for almost an hour. Neither one knew what started the argument.

"This is hurting our daughter!" Sonja lashed out again.

Finally Tom couldn't take any more. "I'm leaving," he shrieked, then slammed the door and left. "Jesus Christ," Tom muttered to himself. "This just isn't working."

He got into his car and sped off. *This isn't how I thought things were going to turn out. I thought there was still hope for our relationship.*

He pulled the car into a parking lot and shut off the engine. Then he buried his face in his hands and sobbed. *My face is really hot*, Tom thought. *My blood pressure must be through the roof.* After a few moments, the flashes of red subsided as the effects of the argument wore off.

He took a few deep breaths, opened his cell phone and called Michael. "Hello, Michael here," came Michael's friendly voice.

"Hey, this is Tom."

Michael knew by the painful undertones of Tom's voice that something was going on. Michael tried to ease the pain he heard in Tom's voice. Then there was silence at the other end of the phone. Michael grew concerned and said louder, "Tom, are you there, are you okay? Where are you?"

"We just had a horrible argument. It was AWFUL." Tom was sniffling, spitting and coughing all at the same time.

"It's going to be okay. Calm down, Tom, let's take a few deep breaths." After a few moments, where Michael could hear Tom taking deep breaths, he said, "So you had a marital discussion. Let's meet somewhere so we can talk this out." They agreed to meet at a nearby coffee shop.

As Michael hung up, he felt a lump growing in his stomach. *Why does life have to be so hard for some people?* He grabbed his work bag, pens, and paper and jumped in his car. Following his advice to Tom, he took a few deep breaths of his own to slow down and headed for the coffee shop. "God please be with me," he said out loud. "I need You to give me words to help my friend."

Minutes later he arrived at the coffee shop and was greeted in the parking lot by a worn-out Tom.

"Geez, I'm glad to see you, Michael." Tom clasped his hand in welcome relief as they entered the coffee shop.

"You want something?" Michael asked.

"Sure, how about some hot green tea?"

"Good choice."

Michael placed their orders at the counter, then joined Tom, who was already seated at a quiet table in the corner.

"Well, what's going on? What happened tonight?" Michael started.

"Well, mister know-it-all, this isn't working. She's never going to change."

Michael paused for a moment, "Before we go on, have you calmed down yet?"

"No. I'm frustrated, hurt and angry."

"Take a deep breath. Try to relax. Let's review. Help me understand what happened."

"I forgot to pay a bill and we got into an argument about it. She started right into me! She won't give me any credit for trying. She just flies off the handle and lets me have it. I couldn't take it anymore, so I got really upset, yelled, slammed the door and drove away. I got to a parking lot and tried to calm down and called you. She is *never* going to change. Never!"

"Tom, I hear and see your frustration," Michael said. "I am so sorry this happened to you."

"Not as sorry as I am," Tom said warily.

Michael moved on, "Was there anything that you did that seemed to work for you?"

"No! Of course not. She won't cooperate. She's...she's just..." Tom was exasperated. He felt himself getting upset again. "Man, oh man, oh man..."

Michael paused to allow Tom to regain his composure. "So, is any of this helping your situation?"

"No, no, it isn't."

"Then why are you still doing the same things? And why are you concentrating on *her* behavior?"

It was as if a hot branding iron had touched Tom's skin. He jerked at the last couple of comments and sat perfectly still, eyes wide.

"Why *am* I doing that?" Michael barely heard Tom's words, his voice was so low.

"Sometimes," Michael said quietly, "People repeat the same behavior until the pain of the present situation becomes greater than the fear of change. Is that you in this example?"

"Yes," Tom whispered.

It finally hit him. They had been meeting for two weeks and this was the "Changing Your Heart" Michael had spoken about. It was no longer just a concept in Tom's head. He had resisted the change, but finally he was ready to surrender to it. He knew at that point he had changed in many areas.

"What happens now?" Tom said.

"First, can you change your wife?"

"No. She has to want to change."

"So what can you do?"

"I can, hmmm...I can create the best possible conditions for Sonja so she will choose to want to restore our relationship. I guess," Tom ventured.

"Are you guessing, or do you know what to do – with your heart?"

"I know."

With compassion in his voice, Michael said, "Tom, let's discuss the ingredients. Right now, what ingredients are you using?"

Tom replied, "I am stepping into integrity. I have forgiven Sonja. I have asked Sonja for forgiveness. The experience with my brother-in-law convinced me this works."

"After tonight, do you think you will have to forgive her and ask for her forgiveness? Because you will, Tom. Don't let anything build up on your list of offenses. Don't let the sun go down on your anger. (Eph 4:26-27)"

"Let's switch subjects, Tom. How are you doing with Sonja's relational needs?"

"Not very well. Can we go over that again?"

"Sure. Relational needs are those needs you have had from the beginning of your life," Michael said, reaching into his bag. Michael continued talking and wrote down each need on a sheet of paper as they went along.

Tom listened intently as Michael explained.

"Take attention, for example. Most young children crave attention. Tom, have you ever had anyone's undivided attention?"

Tom said, "Yes, I had a grandpa whose nickname for me was 'The Little Prince.' When I was around him, I felt as though it was just me and him; there was no one else in the world but me."

"How did that feel?"

Tom replied, "He made me feel special."

"Great example, Tom. Another relational need is listening. Some people just need to be heard. We have a hard time with this since the introduction of cell phones, text messaging and the Internet. Just stop and be with your wife, look into her eyes. Then listen to her."

"It's that simple?"

"Yes, Tom; it is that simple."

"Tell me more about these needs."

"Okay. What does appreciation mean to you, Tom?"

"Well, to me it means being thankful for what you have and what others have done for you."

"You got it, Tom."

"Examples of other relational needs are:

- Uplifting Others: This means giving and receiving support; coming alongside and offering help to others in need.

- Honor and Respect: Most of the time this is a man's greatest need. Being valued and deemed worthy are at the core of this need.

- Affection: This could be words, such as 'I love you.' It is also a touch on the shoulder, stroke of her hand. Here's the most important part of that. When you touch her, it is a touch without a future! It's just affection.

- Protection and security: This is a great need for most women. For instance, it's quite possible that your choice to not pay a bill presented a threat to your wife's home and safety, her sense of stability, so to speak. She felt threatened, her defenses flared up and your defenses flared up and the next thing you know you're having an argument."

Michael continued, "Tom, you need to have Sonja define what her needs look like and sound like. For instance, if one of Sonja's needs is affection, she might want you to tell her that you love her.

"If I asked you to define what affection looks like and sounds like to you, your answer could be different. You might say, 'Sonja, affection to me is you hugging me and telling me you love me.' Different definitions, huh?"

"The list is endless, words of affirmation or entering into another's world. An example of how my wife and I enter into each other's world is she rides in the golf cart while I golf, and I might go shopping with her and be joyous about it."

"Boy, that's a hard one for me. That shopping thing, yuck! Just shoot me," Tom laughed.

"Even though you may not care for the actual activity, has it ever created joy in your spouse when you enjoyed being with her?" Michael asked.

Tom responded, "Yeah, I know what you mean. Last year we shopped for Christmas gifts for our daughter together. My goodness, we had a blast!"

Michael connected the dots for Tom. "Did she have fun?"

"You'd better believe it!"

"What was different, from your normal shopping experience?"

"I really wanted to be there shopping with her."

"Do you suppose it met a relational need for your wife?"

"Yes, probably companionship and approval."

"Did you expect anything in return?"

"Nope, it just happened."

"So supporting your wife by meeting her relational needs accomplished what?"

"Joy and harmony. But won't she take advantage of me?"

"Did she?"

"Actually, no. It was one of the most memorable nights of our married life," Tom admitted.

Michael had a wry smile on his lips, like he had just eaten something delicious and was ready to share it with others. He quietly sipped his iced coffee, allowing Tom's comments to move from his head to his heart.

Finally the dam broke. Tom's tears streamed down his face as he said, "I commit to supporting my wife's relational needs."

There was nothing else to say. Tom slowly drank his tea and Michael stirred the last of his iced coffee, finishing it without a word.

CRROEOCROCRRO

After their embrace, the couple held hands in silence. They wanted to stay close to the tent so they could hear the children when they awakened. Maria whispered, "You are amazing!"

Yes I am, he thought.

She whispered as though the huge trees surrounding them could hear, "Why do people make marriage so difficult?"

"I haven't the faintest idea. But I do know I have hurt you, even though I treasure you."

"I know you have," she said as she cuddled closer to him. "But here's the difference. You then take the steps to heal me and I take the steps to heal you."

Michael smiled. "You're right. Through all our trials and tribulations, we've always reached out to each other, healing each other and becoming as strong as this redwood forest."

"I bless you with power and strength. I bless you with joy. I bless you with vision and clarity." Maria playfully touched her husband. "Tag, you're it!" Then she quickly ran to other side of the tent, secretly hoping he would chase her.

Michael tried to quiet her by putting his finger over his lips with, "Shhhh! You'll wake the kids!"

"And I bless you with slowness," she laughingly fired back.

Michael had run around to the other side of the tent.

"Gotcha!" he said as he grabbed her. As he kissed her on the nose, Michael asked, "Is this a date night?"

"Not until we do this for 30 minutes."

The Ingredient of
Supporting the Relational Needs of Others

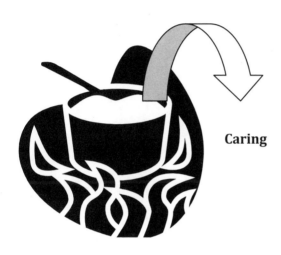

Caring

The Ingredient of **Supporting the Relational Needs of Others** Brings a Sense of Being Cared For.

Support the Relational Needs of Others Worksheet

Discuss the relational needs of others:
A short list is below. *Ask* your spouse, friend, sibling, co-worker, whoever you're in a relationship with, what that person's needs are. Do not guess at this.

Attention

Listening

Appreciation

Uplifting others

Honor

Respect

Affection

Words of affirmation

Entering into that person's world

Support or help

Support the other person by meeting the person's relational needs without expecting your needs to be met. Support each other.

Support the Relational Needs of Others
Worksheet

List or Check the Other Person's Needs:

    Attention

    Listening

    Appreciation

    Uplifting others

    Honor

    Respect

    Affection

    Words of affirmation

    Entering into the other person's world

    Support or help

Other needs:

_____

_____

_____

_____

Support the other person by meeting the other person's relational needs without expecting your needs to be met. Support each other.

CHAPTER 8

Blessing With Your Tongue

Bless those who persecute you;
bless and do not curse. Rom 12:14

"How many times have we uttered a careless word that has damaged our relationship with someone else? Or called someone a name or made fun of their accent? Sadly, I have said horrible words to others, piercing their spirit," Michael admitted in their next meeting.

"In our society, the concept of speaking a blessing over others is diminished. But this doesn't diminish the *power* of speaking a blessing. At one time or another, everyone has encouraged someone with words. Like saying, 'You can do it!' or 'Atta boy!' And we've seen positive results.

Did you play any sports in high school, Tom?"

Tom almost puffed out his chest, "All-State football, wrestling and baseball. I was quite a jock."

Michael nodded. "I was a defensive back on my high school football team. On the weeks when I psyched myself up, you know – 'I'm going to make an interception and I'm going to tackle anyone that comes in my area,' – well, I played a great game. It took me years to figure out that the positive words I said to myself came true. In our relationships, we can't expect *positive* results when we speak *negative* words into our lives and relationships."

"This ingredient is simple; bless with your tongue. It's a key ingredient for lifting others up."

As Michael and Tom sat across from each other, Michael continued, "How much damage have you done with your tongue?"

Tom's head dropped. "More than I care to think about."

"So let's turn that around."

Tom asked Michael, "Does your wife bless you every day? If she does, what does she say?"

Michael thought a moment. "She tells me I have a real cute tush." They both laughed. The laughter did both of their hearts good.

"No really; what else does she say?"

"She says, for instance, 'Honey I bless your hands to produce wealth, I bless your day for doors to open and doors to close, I bless your comings and goings. I bless your life to be a life of influence today.' Things like that."

"And you should bless your wife in the morning and all through the day."

Tom's face crinkled up, "But what if I don't feel like blessing her? In fact, sometimes I feel like doing the opposite."

"Is that helping you?"

"Not really."

"Tom, think about it. What have you got to lose? Will you allow weeds to grow in your relationship because of your pride?"

"Weeds?"

"Remember, you are creating the best possible conditions for the plant that represents your relationship to grow. She gets to choose whether or not she plants the seeds in your relationship. Your lack of heart change and lack of blessing her with your tongue is the equivalent of planting weeds in your relationship."

"Saying blessings at all times will keep those weeds out of the soil. That means healthy growth will be the best possible outcome."

"Say what you want, not necessarily what you have, so that you can have what you want."

"What?" Tom was puzzled. "That sounds like mumbo-jumbo to me."

"How is your relationship with Sonja now?"

"Not good."

"If you keep saying 'not good,' will the relationship get any better?"

"Probably not."

"So Tom, if you chose to 'bless your wife with your tongue,' what do you think will happen?"

"I guess it will get better."

"Then why aren't you blessing your wife with your tongue?"

Tom just stared blankly at Michael.

"Let's practice, Tom. Repeat after me. 'I bless you, Sonja, with health and prosperity today.'"

"I bless you, Sonja, with health and prosperity today."

For the next several minutes, Tom blessed his wife with his tongue.

"Well, how do you feel now?"

"Michael, I feel so much better. Do you think this will work on her?"

"No," Michael replied calmly.

"No? What do you mean?"

"Tom, this isn't about her. This is about you."

"Me?"

"Sure, the blessings you utter about your wife will change your heart toward her. We as human beings can sense when others have good intentions toward us. Your wife will be able to feel the change in you. That change will allow her to choose to replant the seeds that will grow into a healthy relationship between you two."

CRLOLORCRLO

The Ingredient of
Blessing With Your Tongue

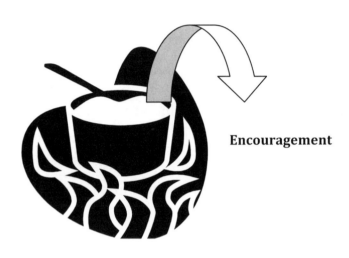

Encouragement

The Ingredient of **Blessing with Your Tongue**
Encourages the Hearts of Others

Blessing With Your Tongue Worksheet

State the positive outcomes you want for the other person such as:

I bless you with abundance.

I bless you with health and physical well-being.

I bless you with peace.

I bless you with healing.

I bless you with joy and laughter.

The opportunities are endless.

Commit to blessing your spouse daily and consistently.

CHAPTER 9

Letting Go

But my sins you let go of, threw them over your shoulder –
good riddance. Is 38:17

"Hey, Tom." Michael greeted Tom. Michael appreciated Tom's positive character quality of punctuality. He had never been late for an appointment. This punctuality in itself showed Tom's determination for getting his relationships back in balance.

"Hello, Michael," Tom said as he sat down and nervously flipped through some papers he had brought with him. "I have a question for you. My question is how do you let go of past hurts?"

Michael paused, collected his thoughts and said, "Have you heard how spider monkeys are caught in the wild?"

"Yes, I've heard the story," Tom answered. "The hunters place the spider monkey's favorite food in a small jar that is anchored down. Once the monkey reaches into the jar and grabs the food, his fist is too big to fit back through the opening. The monkey won't let go of the food, though. That makes it easy for the hunters to capture the monkey."

"In essence the..." Michael started.

Tom finished, "The spider monkey surrenders his freedom because he won't let go of the food."

"How does that apply to you?"

"Well... I hold things in. I don't always share my true feelings with Sonja."

"Why?"

"I guess I feel as though she might hurt me more."

"Tell me why does the spider monkey continue to hold onto something that will ultimately do him harm."

"I don't know, I'm not a spider monkey."

"Take a guess. What do you think the answer would be?"

"I guess the spider monkey doesn't know that he will lose his freedom."

Michael fired back, "I'm sure he knows his hand is stuck in the jar and that he can't move the jar because it is anchored down."

"I suppose you're right. The monkey does know he is stuck. Hmm, perhaps this food is so good that he doesn't think he can get it anywhere else."

"Or..." Michael prompted.

"Or the monkey is just plain stubborn."

"Or..."

"Or he thinks he can get away somehow. Or maybe he wants the food really badly. Or maybe he is stupid. Or he may be greedy."

"Tom, does it really matter why the monkey doesn't let go? No, it doesn't matter because the result is always the same. The monkey loses his freedom."

"Well, how do I let go?"

"Although the technique for catching spider monkeys is probably very successful, I doubt that it is one-hundred percent successful. The monkey that *makes a choice to let go* will remain free. The answer is..."

Tom continued, "I need to make a choice? Choose to let go?"

Michael said. "Yes, it's that simple. I'll show you an exercise to help. Let's get out a piece of paper." Michael handed Tom a blank piece of paper and a pen. Then Michael opened his Bible again, "Here it is. Jesus says, 'Come to me, all of you who are tired of carrying heavy loads, and I will give you rest.' (Matthew 11:28) Jesus will take your load, Tom."

Tom said, "I need something to help me let go. What do I do?"

"You will do what I call a 'paper writing exercise' to help you let go."

"Let's do it."

Michael said, "Write down your past hurts, offenses, anything unpleasant in your past you want to get rid of."

Tom began to write. Soon there were twenty-six items on his list. "Done." Tom said.

"Here's how this works," Michael said. "First, ask God to take this load. These are hurts you have been carrying around inside of you. It sounds like this, 'God take this temper I have, I give it to you.' Go down your list asking God to take each load."

Tom did what Michael asked him to do.

"Next, destroy the list. Shred it. Burn it. Bury it. Get rid of the list."

"Okay." Tom tore the list into little pieces and threw the pieces into a trash can.

"Great," Michael was nearly finished. "This last part is really important."

Tom focused on Michael.

"The next time any of those loads come into your thoughts, you simply say aloud. 'I have given you to God. In fact, you are torn up and in a trash can. You can't come back. Goodbye.' Tom, you *can* let go of the loads, issues, offenses and hurts. Make that choice."

Months Later...

Michael's daughters were in the playground, romping with Tom's daughter. Squeals of joy filled the air as the children enjoyed themselves. Michael and Tom stood on one side of the playground while Maria and Sonja chatted on the other side.

Maria said to Sonja, "Are you doing okay?"

Sonja took a quick peek at her daughter before answering.

"Oh, Maria, we were living a nightmare. But since Tom and Michael began talking, there has been a big change in Tom."

"Like what?"

"To be quite honest, before Tom and Michael talked, Tom was looking at pornography. He lied to me! Can you imagine how painful that was? Oh my God! When I caught him doing that, I felt cheap and dirty. I felt as though he wasn't making love to me, but to one of those, those..." Sonja's voice trailed off and tears began to flow.

Maria waited patiently as a wave of grief washed over Sonja. *Boy*, Maria thought, *a lot of healing took place in their relationship.* Quietly, Maria comforted her friend by just being there.

"I love Tom so much, but before, it was like torture. I wanted him to be with me, but I felt like he was somewhere else. Somewhere dirty, unwholesome and unclean. Thank God Tom went to Michael."

"You were talking about a big change in Tom. Tell me about it, Sonja."

"One night he came home and asked me to forgive him. That was hard for me. Tom vowed to...How did he put it? Oh, yeah. He said he would 'step into integrity.' He told me he would not look at porn and took it off his computer. He even found an 'accountability partner' to help him keep straight."

"Did that help?"

"Yes, it sure did. And I needed help, so I went to a counselor, too."

Sonja radiated confidence, "I really wanted our relationship to work, but I was so hurt. I lashed out at Tom almost every chance I could. I had to learn how to let go of past hurts. The writing exercise Michael showed Tom helped both of us."

Sonja continued, "Slowly and surely, Tom started using Michael's ingredients. The healing that came when Tom asked Andres for forgiveness – Wow, that was powerful. I felt, maybe we could have a chance of restoring our marriage and our relationship."

Sonja paused and looked again at her child. Maria smiled at Michael, who waved at them. The two men appeared to be deep in conversation, with huge grins on their faces. *Almost like the cat that swallowed the canary,* Maria thought. She refocused on Sonja.

"After Tom and Andres had that miraculous recovery, I called my sister, Irene. She confirmed how much it meant to Andres and said they were looking forward to our families getting together again. I know I probably say this too much, but *wow*!"

"Was it all smooth after that?" Maria queried.

"Heck, no. We had another blow-up right after that. I think Michael met Tom at a coffee shop or something like that."

"I remember that, too," said Maria. "Go on."

"After that, Tom always spoke kind and uplifting words to me. They were like cool, clean water in a dry desert to me. He asked for forgiveness again and he kept his word. Then, any time Tom felt that he had hurt me, he was so gentle and loving. He would take my hands, look into my eyes and sincerely ask me to forgive him. He healed me along the way."

From the other side of the playground, while they watched their children play, the two men grinned at each other.

"Michael, what a blessing you are to me and my family. Our lives are so different from that first time we met."

"How?"

Chuckling, and with the biggest smile he could muster, Tom pointed across the playground to his wife, "We're in love again! But this time it's even better!"

"Tom, I'm very proud of you for committing to changing your heart plus engaging the ingredients and weaving them into your life and relationships. I think the results speak for themselves." Michael beamed with delight and waved to Maria. *Atta, girl,* he thought.

Across the playground, Sonja continued, joy radiating from her. "I wanted to know what had caused Tom to change so much." A big grin appeared on her face. "So I contacted Michael and got a copy of the ingredients worksheets. He explained the process to me. Then we met with him a few times and kept using the ingredients in our lives and with others. And just look at us now! We are whole, healthy and helping others. I asked Michael if I could share this with friends. You know him, he just looked at me and smiled."

ରଔଔଔଔ

Letting Go Worksheet

You may want to use a separate piece of paper for this, because you're going to destroy this worksheet once you've completed it.

Describe the offense, issue, hurt, load or burden - and be specific:

_____

_____

_____

_____

_____

_____

_____

_____

_____

_____

_____

_____

_____

_____

CHAPTER 10

Leadership

Love and truth form a good leader; sound leadership is founded on loving integrity. Prov 20:28

Six months after their meeting in the park, Tom and Sonja checked their mail at home. Excited, Sonja opened it and said, "Tom, we've got mail."

They had received a request from Michael. It read: "I am always interested in your progress. Please take some time to write to me and update me on your well-being. I am also interested in knowing how *Changing Your Heart* has affected you in other areas of your life.

"The areas are leadership, change and work-life balance. Be blessed and thank you in advance for your commitment and responses."

The letter was signed by Michael.

Sonja said, "You write about leadership, I'll write about change and we will both write about life-work balance."

"Done," Tom responded.

Tom sat down at his computer and wrote the following note to Michael.

Dear Michael,

Wow. Things have turned around for our marriage and our life as well. We are doing great! We have taken all of the ingredients and we use them in all areas of our life and with everyone we meet.

Leadership:

One of the things I can tell you is that we are all leaders in some form or fashion. At work, especially if you are a manager or some "big shot," there is an opportunity to be a leader. But we all have an opportunity to step into a leadership role. At church, synagogue, mosque, with volunteer organizations like United Way, Boy Scouts, Feeding the Hungry or any religious environment; leadership is always needed.

Since you and I worked together, I have improved in my leadership skills. I am now "Stepping into Integrity" with the people I lead.

I am a person of integrity, so as a leader I can be trusted. Keeping your word goes a long way in providing an atmosphere that's conducive to productivity at home, work, church and even at play.

I read somewhere that a leader can't take people where they aren't willing to go. That means without integrity, I can't lead anyone anywhere but downward. If I do not carry integrity in me, then how can I expect to have anyone I lead to carry integrity in them?

Integrity is like your skin. It can be damaged from over-exposure to life's indulgences just like the skin can become damaged in the sun. We have to live with integrity meshed and molded inside us. We need to let it surround us like our skin. Integrity is with me every day and I want it to be with others as well.

Michael, I cannot express enough gratitude for the incredible turn-around that changing my heart has produced in my family. My heart has truly changed in every facet.

As a leader, we all mess up, say something wrong or make a mistake. Great leaders recognize their mistakes, correct them and move on. Using the ingredients of "Asking for Forgiveness" and "Forgiving Others" are keys for moving forward. I asked not only my wife for forgiveness, but also my fellow employees.

I decided to commit. Then I acted on my decision. Leadership is about acting on your decisions. You and I worked out a plan. And I acted upon the plan. I created a "space," allowing others to follow. My moving forward, in essence, created a vacuum behind me. I invited others to follow and presto! Leadership.

I created that vacuum by moving forward. The vacuum allowed people to choose to join in, because my heart had changed. I cared about others, which in turn brought out the best in them.

Before my "heart change," I talked to my employees because it was something I had to do. I read about it in some managerial book; "Talk to your employees about their personal lives so they can be more productive." I talked to my employees about non-work matters. Check; did it. I'm sure they thought I didn't care. I was just checking off some imaginary box of something I had to do as a manager.

It wasn't effective until my heart changed. Wow, what a positive difference! My change of heart allowed me to "Support the Relational Needs of Others." Sometimes all I needed to do was just listen. Sometimes that was the most important thing I *could* do.

And by listening to my employees, I could assign work based on their strengths and their desires.

I've included a chart to explain this point. The vertical axis represents the person's passion or desire. The horizontal axis represents the person's talent or ability:

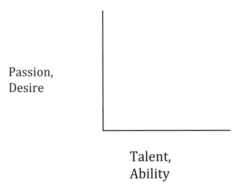

Passion,
Desire

Talent,
Ability

Some people have lots of passion or desire, but little or no talent or ability. Have you seen some of those singing talent search shows on TV? The singers are awful, but they really believe they can sing! So their charts look like the one below:

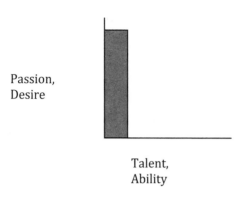

Passion,
Desire

Talent,
Ability

The shaded area represents a person's potential.

The next chart represents a maliciously compliant person who has talent/ability but no passion/desire.

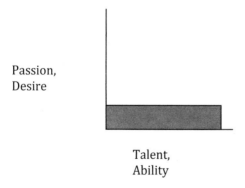

Passion,
Desire

Talent,
Ability

Once again, the shaded area represents a persons' potential.

The next chart is amazing. After I started really listening to my employees, I could match projects with their talent/ability and passion/desire, reaping more productivity because the potential is so much greater, as seen in this chart:

Passion, Desire

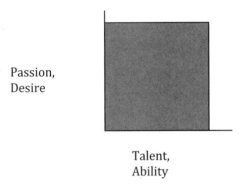

Talent, Ability

Michael, employing my change of heart, mixed with the ingredients you taught me, helped me become a better leader at work, home and in society.

My work is more exciting than ever. I have people where they should be, rather than filling a space that doesn't suit their passion.

I am so glad that – on a scale of one to ten – your passion and desire is a ten. I am just as excited that your talent and ability is the same. You, Michael, are living full in what you were called to do.

Give our love to Maria.
Thanks, Tom

Leadership Worksheet

List some activities that can enhance your leadership skills. Record the date you plan to participate in or complete each activity.

Activity   Date

_____

_____

_____

_____

_____

_____

_____

_____

_____

_____

_____

_____

_____

_____

_____

Leadership Worksheet

List leadership seminars or classes you plan to attend. Record the date you plan to go to the leadership seminar or class.

Seminar/Class   Date

_____

_____

_____

_____

List leadership books you plan to read. Record the date you plan to finish these books.

Book   Date

_____

_____

_____

_____

_____

_____

_____

_____

CHAPTER 11

Change

Do not conform any longer to the pattern of this world, but be
transformed by the renewing of your mind.
Rom 12:2

Sonja wrote her letter to Michael and Maria.

Dear Michael and Maria,

I am responding back to you about change.

Wow! Sometimes it is hard to grasp the concept of
change. But, here goes.

I think many people are afraid of change. Change is a
part of how our world operates. If we don't change,
we'll be left behind.

We've all heard that the dinosaurs couldn't adapt to
rapid change. Now we look at their bones in museums
because dinosaurs are no longer around.

Tom and I have changed for the better. Our relationship has changed for the better. We pause regularly for our marriage meetings. That's a huge change and we are continuing to improve. I love dating Tom again. He invests time in our daughter, Lisa. I have changed as well. I must tell you about a wonderful change in me.

I am a teacher and I taught summer school with another teacher last year. We got paid at the end of the summer. He got the check and he was supposed to share half with me. After the first month, I called him for my portion of the check. He gave me a flimsy excuse about why he couldn't pay me then. It was the same thing the next month.

After six months, I was really frustrated and threatened to hire a lawyer to force him to give me my half. I shared this information in one our marriage meetings and Tom suggested that I forgive the man. Of course, I resisted. Actually, it was major league resistance! Unfortunately, I still go there sometimes. But Tom was persistent with this. So I made a choice to forgive the man and ask him for forgiveness.

The big day came. I went to him and said, "Please forgive me for being rude to you. I forgive you for the way you have acted about the summer school check." I walked out of his office changed and with a huge burden lifted.

Then the next week, a miracle happened. The check arrived in the mail! I was blown away. The change in me, changing my heart, produced a change in his heart.

So as I write to you about change, it is all good.

Adapt or be run over.

Thank you so much for investing in Tom and me.

Blessings,
Sonja

Change Worksheet

List some changes you are going to make. Record the
date you plan to complete each change.

Change   Date

_____

_____

_____

_____

_____

_____

_____

_____

_____

_____

_____

_____

_____

_____

_____

_____

_____

Change Worksheet

List your goals for change and how each change will improve the quality of your relationships.

Goal #1:

_____

_____

How the change will improve the quality of my relationships:

_____

_____

Goal #2:

_____

_____

How the change will improve the quality of my relationships:

_____

_____

Goal #3:

_____

_____

How the change will improve the quality of my relationships:

_____

_____

CHAPTER 12

Life-Work Balance

Whoever wants to be great must become a servant. Whoever wants to be first among you must be your slave. That is what the Son of Man has done: He came to serve, not to be served.
Matt: 20:27-28

Dear Michael and Maria,

Tom and Sonja here. We're responding to your request.

Defining our purpose is one of the keys to creating the type of life-work balance that helped strengthen our marriage. The old proverb, "All work and no play make Jack a dull boy" is certainly true for us.

Together, we've used our marriage meetings to create a wonderful life-work balance. During one of our marriage meetings, we discussed our purpose.

Sonja went first. She defined her purpose as follows:

"I, Sonja, believe my purpose is to be the best mother and wife I can be. I will also support my neighbors when they are in need."

Tom followed:

"I, Tom, believe my purpose is to pay forward the help given to me by my friend Michael – to help marriages become better."

So for us, the effect of this self-discovery aligns with our purpose.

Tom here. I know that I can be a perfectionist at times. I used to put in long hours at work to make sure things were perfect there. Well, this hurt our marriage and it didn't align with my purpose. The phrase "help marriages become better" included my own marriage.

Now, I still perform very well at work, but I don't go overboard, because it takes me away from my purpose.

Sonja agrees that we both have re-assessed how we work, play, worship and socialize. Through our hearts being changed, we have balanced all of those activities.

Sonja here. As a woman, I rarely took vacations. There was too much to do around the house. Now we plan a couple of week-long family vacations each year to rest, play and reenergize.

Oh by the way, Lisa is amazing. I have used a creative method before I play video games with her. Lisa is so good at them, I am not much competition for her. Within seconds I am toast. So I've hidden some of them and I practice when she is not around! I still lose, but at least I'm competitive. She seems to enjoy our 'time' together doing things she likes. (Smiley face) ☺

Tom and I also balance each other. During our marriage meetings, we talk about taking on too much stress. Then we discuss ways to eliminate the stress.

Here are some areas to balance:

Work
Spiritual
Physical
Mental
Play
Family

Work: We made a choice to enjoy the work we do.

Spiritual: Take some time to meditate or pray or maybe get close to nature. We loved your redwood forest stories and we have camped there twice since we last met.

Physical: Tom and I work out together at least once a week. I beat him at racquetball! Okay, that's a joke. We eat foods that are fresh and nutritious to stay healthy.

Mental: Tom and I stay active mentally. We play games and help Lisa with her homework. Kids today learn a lot and quickly.

Play: Yahoo! Our date nights and family vacations are so much fun!

Family: We engage each other as family members. We participate in family reunions, and gain insight from other generations, especially those older than us. As we focus on our family, we have come to enjoy and appreciate each other even more.

Michael and Maria, we will keep in touch.

>*Be balanced. We love you.*
>*Tom and Sonja*

Life-Work Balance Worksheet

Work
Spiritual
Physical
Mental
Play
Family

Work: Enjoy your work.

Spiritual: Take time to meditate, pray or maybe get close to nature.

Physical: Exercise together at least once a week. Eat fresh foods. Eat foods that are nutritious.

Mental: Stay active mentally. Do jigsaw puzzles, math problems, crossword puzzles, play board games and help children with their homework.

Play: Date each other and take vacations.

Family: Schedule family time. Participate in family reunions.

Life-Work Balance Worksheet

Work

What do you enjoy about your work?

_____

_____

_____

What kind of work do you enjoy doing?

_____

_____

_____

How can your purpose and passion align with your work or job?

_____

_____

_____

How can you include fun at work?

_____

_____

_____

Life-Work Balance Worksheet

Spiritual

Do you meditate or pray? List the times and dates of your meditation or prayer.

Meditation/Prayer   Date and time

_____

_____

_____

_____

What do you do that brings you close to nature?

_____

_____

_____

When will you do activities to bring you close to nature?

Activity   Date

_____

_____

_____

Life-Work Balance Worksheet

Physical

What physical activities do you do? List the activities and dates you participate in them.

Activity   Date

_____

_____

_____

_____

_____

_____

Write down how you monitor your eating habits.

_____

_____

_____

_____

_____

_____

_____

_____

Life-Work Balance Worksheet

Mental

Here is a short list of mental activities:

Jigsaw puzzles

Su Doku puzzles

Math problems

Crossword puzzles

Board games

Help children with homework

What mental activities do you do? List the activities and dates.

Activity   Date

_____

_____

_____

_____

_____

_____

_____

Life-Work Balance Worksheet

Play

List the vacations you're planning and dates you plan to go.

Vacations   Date

_____

_____

_____

_____

_____

_____

List activities and dates for your date nights.

Activity   Date

_____

_____

_____

_____

_____

_____

Life-Work Balance Worksheet

Family

List family activities and dates.

Activity   Date

_____

_____

_____

_____

_____

_____

_____

Plan to attend a family reunion.

_____

_____

_____

_____

_____

_____

_____

ABOUT THE AUTHORS

Richmond and Debbie Caldwell were married in January 1987 and have personally experienced the pain of divorce. They were determined not to let anyone else go through the unnecessary steps of divorce, so they began extensive studies in restoring marriage in all areas of "brokenness."

They are teachers, dynamic speakers and coaches who have taught marriage classes since 2000. They have spoken at marriage seminars and are known for their highly effective and dynamic style – and results. Richmond graduated from the U.S. Air Force Academy and has flown extensively around the world. He graduated with top honors from the Navigator Instructor School and was selected Navigator Instructor of the Year. Richmond is a certified facilitator of Stephen Covey's Seven Habits, Achieve Global and Coaching for Performance. He is a gifted motivational speaker and has garnered countless awards as a member of Toastmasters International.

Debbie attended the University of Texas San Antonio. She has helped numerous families achieve healing in life through Family Coaching, where she served as Fort Worth Area Director until March 2008. She is a gifted speaker and speaks on a regular basis to groups in the Dallas-Fort Worth area.

Richmond and Debbie have lived all over the world. They now reside in Fort Worth, Texas with their two daughters, Courtney and Alyeska. They have three grown sons, Christopher, Nicholas and Adam.

Other Books by the Authors:

Changing Your Heart: How to Enhance, Rekindle, Repair and Restore Relationships

Staying Hitched, It's Not As Hard As You Think!

Staying Hitched, the Workbook

For more information contact:
Richmond and Debbie at 817-292-1120

ABOUT RANDD ENTERPRISES

After eight years of teaching, speaking and coaching, Richmond and Debbie Caldwell launched Randd Enterprises in 2008.

The mission of Randd Enterprises is to bring healing into the lives of others through teaching, consulting, coaching, workshops, speaking and books. We don't heal anyone. God does that. We have found that couples who apply the principles we teach have what we call the ShaZamm result! God blesses their marriages and we are privileged to see His miracles.

We also teach pre-married couples. Who better to show them how to be married than a happily married couple? The principles we share give pre-married couples a road map for the rest of their marriage. Our teachings have helped many couples heal a lot of their "junk" before they drag it into their marriage.

We also teach an eight-week marriage course called Staying Hitched.

www.ChangingYourHeart.com

SUGGESTED READING

The Holy Bible

The Joy of Marriage God's Way, Beverly LaHaye

Liberated Through Submission, P.B. Wilson

Rekindled, Pat and Jill Williams

Creative Counterpart, Linda Dillow

Wild at Heart, John Eldredge

Laugh Your Way to a Better Marriage, Mark Gungor

The Pursuit of Intimacy, Ferguson and Thurman

Power Play, Mike Brock

Creating Your Own Destiny, Patrick Snow

Leadership and Self Deception, The Arbinger Institute

Compassionate Samurai, Brian Klemmer